Literary Newsmakers for Students, Volume 1

Project Editor
Anne Marie Hacht **Editorial**
Sara Constantakis and Ira Mark Milne **Rights Acquisition and Management**
Margaret Chamberlain-Gaston and Sue Rudolph **Manufacturing**
Drew Kalasky

Imaging
Lezlie Light, Mike Logusz, and Kelly Quin **Product Design**
Pamela A. E. Galbreath **Vendor Administration**
Civie Green **Product Manager**
Meggin Condino © 2006 Gale, a part of Cengage Learning Inc.

For more information, contact
Gale, an imprint of Cengage Learning

27500 Drake Rd.

Farmington Hills, MI 48331-3535

Or you can visit our internet site at http://www.gale.com **ALL RIGHTS RESERVED**
No part of this work covered by the copyright herein may be reproduced or used in any form or by any means—graphic, electronic, or mechanical, including photocopying, recording, taping, Web distribution, or information storage retrieval systems—without the written permission of the publisher.

For permission to use material from the product, submit your request via the Web at http://www.gale-edit.com/permissions, or you may download our Permissions Request form and submit your request by fax or mail to: *Permissions Department*
Gale, an imprint of Cengage Learning

27500 Drake Rd.

Farmington Hills, MI 48331-3535

Permissions Hotline:

248-699-8006 or 800-877-4253, ext. 8006

Fax: 248-699-8074 or 800-762-4058

Since this page cannot legibly accommodate all copyright notices, the acknowledgments constitute an extension of the copyright notice.

While every effort has been made to secure permission to reprint material and to ensure the reliability of the information presented in this publication, Gale, an imprint of Cengage Learning neither guarantees the accuracy of the data contained herein nor assumes any responsibility for errors, omissions or discrepancies. Gale, an imprint of Cengage Learning accepts no payment for listing; and inclusion in the publication of any organization, agency, institution, publication, service, or individual does not imply endorsement of the editors or publisher. Errors brought to the attention of the publisher and verified to the satisfaction of the publisher will be corrected in future editions.

ISBN 1414402813
ISSN 1559-9639

Printed in the United States of America

10 9 8 7 6 5 4 3 2 1

True History of the Kelly Gang

Peter Carey

2000

Introduction

Since the publication in 1974 of *The Fat Man in History*, Australian novelist and short story writer Peter Carey has often played with the literal truth, blurring the line between history and fiction and combining fact with fable. *True History of the Kelly Gang* (2000) is no different. It is the fictional first-person account of Ned Kelly, the notorious nineteenth-century bushranger and outlaw who is as well-known to Australians, and as fascinating to them, as Jesse James is to Americans or Robin Hood is to the English.

In *True History of the Kelly Gang*, Kelly is writing a series of letters to his unborn daughter. In these letters, he attempts to explain why he first became an outlaw—because he had no choice, he says—and provide her with a true history because, he explains, he knows "what it is to be raised on lies and silences." His own father was an Irish convict, shipped along with his mother to Australia during the Great Transportation. The past has long been dead or silenced for the transported, as if the memory of what was left behind is too painful to talk about. Kelly himself is painfully aware of what that means for him and his culture: they are a people with no cultural memory, adrift, rootless, and left without any meaningful future.

Kelly's "letters" are urgent, raw, and largely unpunctuated, but they are vivid and uniquely written. He speaks the rough language of an Irish Australian and makes easy references to stories and myths that might be lost on a contemporary audience—or on the daughter whom he addresses— if Carey were not so careful to place them in context. Carey's decision to write Kelly's story in Kelly's voice gives readers an opportunity to understand the man behind the legend.

Author Biography

Peter Carey was born May 7, 1943, in the town of Bacchus Marsh in the Australian state of Victoria. He was the youngest of three children, and his parents, Percival Stanley and Helen Jean Carey, owned and operated a local automobile dealership. Carey attended Geelong Grammar School, a private school, and enrolled in a science program at Monash University in 1961. He performed poorly there and left after his first year. In 1962, he took a job as an advertising copywriter in Melbourne, and in 1964, married Leigh Weetman. From 1967 to 1970, Carey lived in London and traveled throughout Europe. Between the time he left Monash University in the early 1960s until he left London at the beginning of the 1970s, he had finished three novels that were never published. He returned to Melbourne and took another job in advertising. In 1973, he finished a fourth novel that was accepted for publication, but Carey withdrew it before it went to press.

That same year, Carey and Weetman separated, but his career as a writer was about to take off. In 1974, his first book of short stories, *The Fat Man in History*, was published by the University of Queensland Press and earned Carey critical praise as well as an enthusiastic readership. Shortly after the book's publication, Carey moved yet again, this time from Melbourne to Sydney for a senior position in advertising. In 1977, Carey published another book of short stories, *War Crimes*, which established him as an important young writer on the Australian literary scene. It also established his signature style; he writes with a dark humor, often twists historical events, and includes absurd elements in otherwise realistic tales. *Bliss*, Carey's first novel, followed in 1981, and he adapted it for a film version, which was released in 1985. In that same year, Carey married theater director Alison Summers.

Since then, Carey has published nine more novels, including: *Illywhacker* (1985); *Oscar and Lucinda* (1988), for which Carey won England's Booker Prize, and which became a motion picture starring Ralph Fiennes and Cate Blanchett; *The Big Bazoolhey* (1995), a children's novel; *Jack Maggs* (1997), a reworking of Charles Dickens's *Great Expectations; True History of the Kelly Gang* (2000), which earned Carey his second Booker Prize; *My Life as a Fake* (2003); and *Wrong About Japan: A Father's Journey with His Son* (2005), a nonfiction account about a trip to Japan with his twelve-year-old son. Additionally, in 1992 he wrote the screenplay for German director Wim Wenders's *Until the End of the World*, and he has taught writing at New York University and Princeton University.

Plot Summary

Prologue

True History of the Kelly Gang opens with an anonymous and handwritten third-person account of Kelly and his gang's last stand in the town of Glenrowan. Kelly himself provokes the battle at Glenrowan when he lures the police, or the "traps," into a shootout. The account describes the moment that defines Kelly in the Australian imagination: Kelly and his boys appear on a hotel veranda, clad in homemade body armor and bucket-shaped helmets, and Kelly declares himself "The Monitor," after a famous iron-sided battleship in service during the American Civil War. The document has an acquisition number and purports to be housed in the Melbourne Public Library, which serves to establish historical authenticity.

Parcel 1: His Life until the Age of 12

Shortly before the end of his career, the historical Kelly composed what has come to be called the "Jerilderie Letter," an 8300-word account of his life, his motivations, and his hopes for the future; which he wanted to have printed in a newspaper, any newspaper. The document was lost or ignored and was never made available to the public, which infuriated Kelly. The *True History of the Kelly Gang* alleges to be Kelly's second effort as an author, a series of letters to his unborn daughter that "will contain no single lie may I burn in Hell if I speak false."

Kelly begins his tale with the transportation of his father, John "Red" Kelly, from Ireland to Van Dieman's Land, a small island near Australia known today as Tasmania, for crimes about which Kelly never heard his father speak. Constable O'Neill, a sinister representative of the local police, tells Ned Kelly a story about "A Certain Man," who plotted with others back in Ireland to murder a landowner whose policies they thought unfair. Eventually, this "Certain Man" was caught and transported to Van Dieman's land. Kelly understands this Certain Man" to be his father. Later, O'Neill tells Kelly about the night he saw Red Kelly wearing a dress, which Kelly does not believe until he accidentally finds the dress, exactly as it was described by O'Neill, buried in a metal trunk.

Kelly depicts his mother, Ellen Kelly, as resolute and tough. She alternately fights with and entertains the police in her home. She stands up to the law for her family, above all else. Late in Parcel 1, Kelly commits his own first crime when he kills a neighboring farmer's calf to put food on the Kelly table. Despite Kelly's admissions of guilt, his father is arrested and jailed for poaching, and he later dies as a result of his stay in prison.

Parcel 2: His Life Ages 12-15

Kelly's family, led by their mother, moves to Greta, leaving Kelly and his brother Jem behind to work for their mother's sisters. After the arrest of her brother James and other injustices, Ellen Kelly's dreams of a more prosperous future are dashed. Now that her husband is dead, Ellen Kelly begins to take a number of unsavory suitors.

Harry Power, a bushranger and outlaw, appears at the Kelly's one night. He becomes one of Ellen Kelly's suitors briefly, and then he becomes Ned Kelly's mentor. Power has escaped from Pentridge Prison, where he knew Ellen Kelly's brother James, and he gives Ellen Kelly money to hire a better lawyer for him. Kelly and Jem follow their mother, sisters, and little brother to Greta.

Kelly reveals that Ellen Kelly's dream of fertile land, domestic peace, and a prosperous, legitimate livelihood have taken root in him as well. It is, he will later insist, all he ever wanted. Writing directly to his unborn daughter, he tells her that Ellen Kelly's new house is where she will eventually be conceived.

Parcel 3: His Life at 15 Years of Age

At the wedding of his sister Annie to yet another troublemaker, Alex Gunn, Kelly sees his mother dancing with a "ferret faced fellow" named Bill Frost. He is disturbed by his mother's gay and girlish behavior in Frost's presence. During the reception, Power appears and lures Kelly away for what Kelly believes will be a brief excursion on horseback. In fact, it is the beginning of his apprenticeship to Power.

Kelly and Power ride into the bush to Power's hideout on Bullock Creek, in the Wombat Mountain Range. Soon, Kelly is Power's accomplice in a stagecoach robbery, and though all they manage to get from the robbery is some lace, an English clock, and a bag full of marbles, his fate as an outlaw is sealed: "that was the moment ... I made myself a bushranger as well."

Following a fight with one of Power's friends, Kelly is sent home, where he finds that Frost has moved in. He also discovers that his mother has betrayed him and sold him into servitude to Power. The police come for Kelly, to arrest him for his part in the robbery of Chinese merchant Ah Fook, but Power arrives in time to pay Kelly's bail.

Parcel 4: His Life at 16 Years of Age

Not long after Kelly learns his mother is carrying Frost's child, Power arrives at Ellen Kelly's home to claim the merchandise he has paid for: her son Ned Kelly. As soon as Kelly rides off into the bush with Power, Frost abandons Ellen Kelly. When Kelly finds out about it from Power, he vows to murder Frost.

Kelly and Power pass through a hellish brushfire as they search for Frost, whom they find with a prostitute. Kelly shoots Frost in the stomach with his rifle and leaves him for dead on the steps of the whorehouse. Later, and despite knowledge to the contrary, Power assures Kelly that Frost did indeed die of his gunshot wounds.

Following the robbery of R. R. McBean, a powerful landowner, Power and Kelly travel to Tambo Crossing, seeking the safety of anonymity. Frost makes a surprise reappearance and tells Kelly that Power has been, and continues to be, involved with his mother, too. In a blind rage, Kelly almost kills Power, steals his beloved horse Daylight, and embarks on a journey into the bush.

Parcel 5: His Early Contact with Senior Policemen

Kelly returns home, meets his new baby sister Ellen, and learns that the town of Greta is crawling with police, who soon arrest him for his connections to Power and the McBean robbery. As he learns more about what he can expect from the police and the wealthy from increased interactions with them, Kelly's growing awareness of English injustices against the Irish is made plain.

Tricked into a fistfight for his freedom by police commissioners who want to capture Power, Kelly wins the fight but is returned to a jail cell when he refuses to betray Power. His opponent in the fight, Constable John Fitzpatrick, befriends

Kelly and warns him that Kelly's uncle Jack Lloyd is about to turn in Power for the reward money.

When Kelly is released from prison as Power is taken into custody, everyone, including his mother, takes it as a sign that Kelly, and not Lloyd, turned in Power to secure his own release. Kelly becomes a pariah, or outcast, in the community, and two of his other uncles, Jimmy and Pat Quinn, are among the most upset.

Parcel 6: Events Precipitated by the Arrest of Harry Power

Another former prisoner of Van Dieman's Land, Ben Gould, a traveling salesman of sorts, arrives with his cart of housewares at the Kelly place. He has a broken-down horse that he says belongs to the McCormicks, a husband and wife in the same line of work as Gould. What Gould does not say is that the horse is stolen, and that Gould harbors a passionate hatred of Mr. McCormick, who was a warden at Van Dieman's Land.

The McCormicks, following a humiliating confrontation with Gould, get their horse back and retreat to town, where Kelly delivers them a Mafia-like message from Gould: a pair of sheep testicles wrapped in cloth with a note telling McCormick he will need them in bed with Mrs. McCormick.

Constable Hall feels himself betrayed by Kelly in an earlier public confrontation with his uncles Jimmy and Pat, an outgrowth of the Power arrest.

Though he once promised to watch out for Kelly, he manufactures the false charge of horse theft that sends Kelly to prison for three years.

Parcel 7: His Life Following His Later Release from Pentridge Gaol

When Kelly is released from prison, he returns to his mother's house once again, and once again he is disappointed to find that Ellen Kelly has not only taken another unsuitable husband, George King, who is Kelly's age, but that she has had King's child. Kelly, who has come home to save the farm, laments, "All my life all I wanted were a home." He finds that King, who wants to get into the horse-thieving business, is a bad influence.

Kelly takes a job at a sawmill—the first real job he has ever had—but cannot forget about Wild Wright, whom he believes was instrumental in the betrayal that sent him to prison. Seeing an opportunity, a pub owner talks Kelly out of a street fight with Wright in favor of a boxing match. Kelly's narration of the brawl is bloody and once again underscores English mistreatment of the Irish.

By the end of this chapter, Kelly is living a quiet life, working at the sawmill, breeding horses with his cousin Tom Lloyd, and cultivating his literary side. His friend Joe Byrne has given him a Bible, some Shakespeare, and a copy of *Lorna Doone*, which Kelly reads three times in two years, and which he especially loves for the parallels in the story to his own life.

Parcel 8: 24 Years

Kelly's horse is impounded when it wanders onto former common ground now controlled by the wealthy landowner McBean, and Kelly simply walks into the impoundment lot and retrieves it. When he is accused of horse stealing, he quits his job at the sawmill and heads for Power's old hideout at Bullock Creek. The poet and opium addict Byrne soon shows up, as do Kelly's younger brother Dan and his friend Steve Hart. Hart loves old tales and songs of the Irish rebels, and like Kelly's father, he sometimes wears a woman's frock.

The new constable, Alex Fitzpatrick, turns out to be the brother of John Fitzpatrick, whom Kelly had fought and then befriended in Melbourne. One night, Alex introduces Kelly to Mary Hearn, who will become Kelly's lover and mother to the daughter he addresses in his letters.

Alex Fitzpatrick betrays Kelly by courting his fourteen-year-old sister, Kate. Fitzpatrick has two other women—one of them pregnant—in other towns. In a confrontation on the Kelly porch, Ellen Kelly bashes Fitzpatrick over the head with a shovel and Kelly shoots him in the wrist. Kelly flees for Bullock Creek an outlaw.

Parcel 9: The Murders at Stringybark Creek

In Kelly's absence, the police arrest his mother and take away her baby. She is detained in

Beechworth Prison as an accomplice to her son's shooting of Alex Fitzpatrick. Fitzpatrick then tries to persuade Mary Hearn to turn Kelly in. Meanwhile, to Kelly's unease, the Kelly Gang continues to grow; as Jimmy Quinn, Wild Wright, and Aaron Sherritt, Byrne's lifelong friend and fellow opium addict, arrive.

A manhunt begins, and there is ample evidence that the police intend to bring the Kelly Gang in dead. Kelly and the others get wind of this as they prepare to defend themselves at a hideout on Stringybark Creek. When the police arrive, Kelly and his gang are prepared to ambush them, and three policemen die in the ensuing violence. The gang's reputation grows among the poor, even as they are hunted as outlaw killers by the law.

In retreat and crossing the flood-swollen Murray River on horseback, Kelly's beloved copy of *Lorna Doone* is ruined. Byrne suggests that he, Kelly, and Mary Hearn flee to California, but Kelly is determined to return to his family's home in Greta. He is also determined to free his mother from prison.

Parcel 10: The History Is Commenced

When Kelly arrives in Greta, he discovers that a modified version of events has made the newspapers, and he stays up all night telling Hearn how it really happened. She encourages him to write it all down and tells him she is pregnant with his daughter.

In the aftermath of the shootout on Stringybark Creek, Donald Cameron, a member of Parliament, wonders publicly if the police were not to blame. This provides further motivation for Kelly to write the true version of his story. Hearn, who was born and raised in Ireland, tells Kelly, Dan Kelly, and Hart the story of the Sons of Sieve, Irish rebels who wore women's dresses and smeared their faces with ash to frighten unjust landowners—precisely the activity for which Red Kelly was sentenced to Van Dieman's Land. Kelly reflects on the horror of transporting Irish prisoners to Van Dieman's Land. He feels that those who were transported would rather forget the past, while Kelly and the others of his generation are "left alone ignorant as tadpoles spawned in puddles on the moon."

Having written his story just as Hearn asked him to and hoping to influence the disposition of his case, Kelly sends his long narrative to the Melbourne newspaper for publication. He also comes to the realization that the sympathy of the poor can be bought—just as his uncle sold out Power—and hatches a plan to rob a bank at Euroa, an act that will enhance the Kelly Gang's growing legend and ensure their status as folk heroes.

Parcel 11: His Life at 25 Years of Age

The authorities' manhunt in Kelly's home district widens and twenty-one men are arrested for simply knowing Kelly, including Jack McMonigle, who is well-known for having publicly denounced Kelly. Kelly and his men set out to do chores and help out on the farms of the twenty-one arrested men while they are in jail. Kelly determines that in addition to freeing his mother, he must liberate these newly imprisoned men as well.

Just as Byrne did earlier, Hearn tries to talk Kelly into fleeing with her to California, but he will not leave as long as his mother and the twenty-one men still languish in jail. Hearn boards a ship for California without him.

Kelly grows angry when he realizes the newspaper is not going to print his long letter, so he composes another; this one for government officials. Even without the newspapers to spread it, Kelly realizes his renown is growing: "I were the terror of the government being brung to life in the cauldron of the night."

Parcel 12: Conception and Construction of Armour

With the police drawing nearer and Kelly feeling increasingly pressured, Hearne sends word that Kelly's daughter has been born in San Francisco. Perhaps as a reaction to the birth, Kelly's vision broadens—now he decides he will have to free not only his mother and the twenty-one men from prison, but all "the innocents" as well.

With the authorities on his heels, Kelly heads

to an abandoned shepherd's cabin in the bush. The walls of the cabin are papered over with old newspapers, some of them from the time of the American Civil War, which ended fifteen years before. Alone and bored, Kelly begins reading the newspapers. One story captures his attention: the story of a titanic battle between two ironclad battleships, the Union's USS *Monitor* and Southern States' CSS *Virginia*. Kelly realizes almost at once that men could be ironclad too and become "Soldier[s] of Future Time," or "our 1st Monitor." He organizes and outfits a makeshift forge and foundry, where he and his men are soon banging iron into breastplates, leg-protectors, and the bucket-shaped helmets for which they will be best remembered. In the weeks that follow, they make a number of ironclad suits for local farmers, other men "perjured against and falsely gaoled."

Parcel 13: His Life at 26 Years of Age

Bearing their iron suits, Kelly and his gang arrive in the town of Glenrowan, where Kelly has lured the police and where he will make his last stand on what he calls "[t]his historic night." The ironclad men set up headquarters in a hotel and tavern. They take dozens of hostages, who end up having such a good time with the Kelly gang that when given a chance to escape, only one—a constable—flees.

Outside, Kelly meets school teacher Thomas

Curnow as he arrives into town by buggy and takes him hostage. Curnow—nervous, effeminate "prim & superior"—is carrying a thick copy of the plays of William Shakespeare, and Kelly takes it from him. Curnow is surprised to discover that the outlaw knows the work of the Bard, as Shakespeare is called. Later, Curnow interrupts Kelly as he works on his personal history, and is even more surprised to discover that Kelly is an author. Curnow asks him if he knows *Lorna Doone*, which produces a flood of memories and feelings in Kelly. *Lorna Doone*, of course, is Kelly's favorite book. Seeming to slip into character, Curnow recites the opening passage of *Lorna Doone* from memory, and then, after Kelly lets him read a page of his manuscript, he offers to help Kelly with his five-hundred-page "history."

That night, the Kelly Gang sings, dances, and drinks with their hostages. Kelly is clearly intrigued at the idea of Curnow helping with his manuscript, although Curnow insists he would have to take the manuscript home with him to do Kelly's work justice. This is the end of Kelly's narration, if not quite his story.

"The Siege at Glenrowan" and "The Death of Edward Kelly"

Because Curnow has talked Kelly into handing over his manuscript, Kelly's narration comes to an end. These two brief chapters recount, in the third person, the gang's last hours and Kelly's execution.

With Kelly's five hundred handwritten pages under his arm, Curnow hurries home, deposits the manuscript, and then runs to the railroad tracks to stop the train carrying the group of policemen that Kelly has lured into Glenrowan. Curnow tells them that the Kelly Gang is waiting for them. The police, armed with this information as well as with Webley and Enfield rifles and buckets of deadly Martini-Henry bullets, surround the hotel. Once the shooting begins, the police fire indiscriminately, killing local men, women, and children. Byrne is killed when one of the bullets pierces his armor. Many bullets are deflected off Kelly's armor, but he is eventually wounded and captured. Dan Kelly and Hart stay on and fight until they are burned alive inside the hotel.

Curnow is taken into protective custody in Melbourne and never quite becomes the Australian hero he believes he should be. He keeps the manuscript, despite his often-voiced low opinion of Kelly, and numerous pencil markings on the manuscript seem to prove that he continued to work obsessively on it for years.

Kelly is taken to the Melbourne jail, where he will await his execution. As he mounts the hanging scaffold, his last words are, "Such is life." His final requests are for the release of his mother from prison and that he be buried in consecrated ground. Neither is honored, and he is buried inside the walls of the prison.

Characters

Sir Redmond Barry

Barry is the judge to whom Kelly offers surrender in exchange for dropping the charges against Ellen Kelly. Barry refuses and sentences Ellen to three years in prison.

Joe Byrne

At Kelly's boxing match with Wild Wright, Joe Byrne approaches him and tries to strike up a friendship. He gives Kelly a copy of the novel *Lorna Doone*, a story that has striking parallels to Kelly's own life, and it becomes his favorite book. Later Byrne and Kelly do strike up a friendship, and Byrne becomes the most indispensable member of Kelly's gang. Byrne is an opium addict, however, and his habit brings him into regular contact with a childhood friend, Aaron Sherritt, whom Kelly mistrusts and who later betrays Byrne and Kelly to the police.

Mr. Donald Cameron

Cameron is a member of the Australian parliament. After the incident at Stringybark Creek, he raises questions about whether the police themselves were at fault and caused the massacre.

Thomas Curnow

Curnow is a schoolteacher who becomes one of the Kelly Gang's hostages in Glenrowan. His appearance in the novel is brief but crucial. After Curnow flatters Kelly and convinces him to turn over the "parcels" of his personal history on which he is hard at work—even as the hostages are being held at Mrs. Jones's pub—Curnow is revealed to loathe Kelly and his gang and to hold Kelly's writing in the lowest contempt. Nevertheless, evidence suggests it is Curnow who is responsible for the parcels' survival, and that the schoolteacher even worked on organizing and editing them over the many years that Kelly's work was in his possession.

Constable Alex Fitzpatrick

Fitzpatrick befriends Kelly after hearing of him through his brother John, a constable in Melbourne. He introduces Kelly to Mary Hearn, who will give birth to the daughter to whom Kelly's letters are addressed. Later, Fitzpatrick falls in love with Kelly's fourteen-year-old sister Kate, for which Kelly shoots him in the wrist. Fitzpatrick then betrays Kelly to the police, setting off the novel's final manhunt.

Constable John Fitzpatrick

Constable Fitzpatrick fights Kelly in Melbourne Prison and then befriends him, bringing a whole leg of lamb to Kelly's cell. Later, Fitzpatrick's brother Alex will befriend—and then betray—Kelly as well.

Media Adaptations

- The 2003 movie *Ned Kelly* portrays the legendary story of Kelly and his gang. The movie was adapted from a novel about Kelly by Australian writer Robert Drewe. It stars Heath Ledger as Ned Kelly and Orlando Bloom as fellow gang member Joe Byrne. It is available on DVD from Universal Home Entertainment.

- *True History of the Kelly Gang* (2001) was released in an unabridged version on audio cassette by Audiobooks. It is narrated by Gianfranco Negroponte.

Constable Flood

Flood impregnates Kelly's sister Annie Gunn while her husband Alex is in jail.

Ah Fook

Fook is a Chinese merchant. He is present for the first stagecoach robbery that Kelly and Power attempt together. Power slices open Fook's carpetbag full of marbles, which Kelly takes with him. Fook comes to Kelly's house and has him arrested for highway robbery.

Bill Frost

Bill Frost becomes Ellen's second husband, and he disappears when she becomes pregnant. With Harry Power's help, the sixteen-year-old Kelly hunts Frost down, shoots him, and mistakenly believes he has killed him.

Ben Gould

Gould is a hawker, a traveling salesman who does business from a wagon. Gould involves Kelly in an argument that leads to a jail sentence for Kelly.

Alex Gunn

Gunn appears at the Kelly house, and although Kelly and Annie believe he is one of their mother's suitors, he ends up marrying Annie. Later, he goes to prison for stealing sheep.

Mr. Gill

Mr. Gill is the editor of the Jerilderie *Gazette*. After Kelly writes a long explanation of his actions, he gives it to Gill to print. Kelly hopes his fifty-eight-page letter will exonerate him, or at least force the authorities to release his mother. Gill does not print the letter but gives it to the police instead.

Superintendent Hare

Hare interrogates Kelly in Melbourne, playing the bad cop to his partner Nicolson's good cop.

Steve Hart

Hart is a member of the Kelly Gang and Dan Kelly's best friend. He sometimes wears a dress, as Red Kelly is reported to have done, and he knows it has something to do with the Irish rebels he worships. He does not exactly understand what the dresses are about until Mary, who grew up in Ireland, tells him the story of the Sons of Sieve, who wore dresses and smeared their faces with ashes to frighten their opponents.

Mary Hearn

Alex Fitzpatrick introduces Kelly to Hearn, and Kelly falls in love with her at first sight. She has a child with George King, although Kelly does not know that King is the father. She becomes pregnant again, with the daughter who Kelly addresses in the book. Later she tries to convince Kelly to escape with her to California. He does not, but Hearn makes it to safety in San Francisco where she gives birth to their daughter.

Mr. Irving

Mr. Irving is Kelly's cruel teacher, who makes Kelly dread school and feel shame at his ignorance.

Mrs. Jones

Mrs. Jones runs the tavern where the Kelly Gang holds their hostages during the final showdown at Glenrowan.

Annie Kelly

Annie is Kelly's older sister by one year. She marries Alex Gunn, who later goes to prison. Annie dies in childbirth.

Dan Kelly

Dan Kelly is Ned Kelly's younger brother, and he is the sibling who is most similar to Kelly in temperament. When Kelly sees Dan drunk with some rowdy young men, he tries to make Dan a partner in his legitimate horse business. Later, Dan joins Kelly in what becomes known as the Kelly Gang, and he dies in the hotel fire that occurs during the final standoff with police in Glenrowan.

Edward Kelly

See Ned Kelly

Ellen Quinn Kelly

Throughout most of *True History of the Kelly Gang*, Kelly's mother Ellen is at the center of her son's world. His devotion to her provokes his jealousy of her many lovers, particularly George King, who is Kelly's age. Kelly's loyalty to his mother compels him to defer to her unreasonable—even outrageous—demands, and ultimately leads to his armored last stand at Glenrowan. Ellen is a Quinn—the Quinns are a family of petty thieves and brawlers—and in her own way she is as defiant and difficult as any of them. Nevertheless, Kelly is tireless in his efforts to help her and dies in a vain attempt to free her from prison.

Ellen Quinn

Ellen is also the name Kelly's mother gives to the daughter she has with the scoundrel Bill Frost. Baby Ellen dies at fourteen months.

Gracie Kelly

Gracie is Kelly's sister.

Jem Kelly

Jem is Kelly's younger brother by a year. Jem is not the troublemaker that his male siblings, cousins, and uncles are, though he is willing to stand up for himself and his family.

John Kelly

See Red Kelly

Kate Kelly

Kate is Kelly's little sister. Constable Alex Fitzpatrick falls in love with her, which sets off a series of events that end with a warrant for Kelly's arrest and Ellen Kelly's imprisonment.

Maggie Kelly

Maggie is Kelly's younger sister. She marries Bill Skilling.

Ned Kelly

Ned Kelly is the leader and namesake of the Kelly Gang and the narrator of almost the entire novel, which is presented as a series of personally written "parcels" to his unborn daughter, and covers the period of Kelly's life from age twelve to his execution at twenty-six. He is born into an Irish

Australian family of hardscrabble dirt ranchers, brawlers, and petty thieves who are in near-perpetual conflict with the local landowners, or squatters, and the authorities; who are either English or otherwise represent English, as opposed to Irish, interests. After his father dies, his mother Ellen Kelly apprentices the fifteen-year-old Kelly, for a price, to the bushranger and outlaw Harry Power, who mentors the young man in the ways of banditry, evasion, and a scavenging life in the bush. This apprenticeship sets in motion the currents that will direct Kelly's life thereafter.

As an adult with several prison stints under his belt, Kelly is a natural leader of men. He is by turns tender and brutal, compassionate and ruthless, understanding and remorseless. He will never turn against an ally, and he is a compelling storyteller who is unusually sensitive to language. Kelly repeatedly tells his reader that his life could have been quite different; that all he ever wanted was a piece of land to work, security for his family, and to be left alone. Although there are times when he seems unable to understand himself or his mother, his insights into others—their motives, their innermost fears, and the desires that force them to action—are often piercingly exact. Kelly falls within the camp of folk heroes that includes both Jesse James and Robin Hood.

Red Kelly

Red Kelly is Kelly's father. An Irishman, he is

arrested and transported to Van Dieman's Land, an island prison, for crimes Kelly never heard him talk about. Early in the novel, Constable O'Neill tells Kelly the story of "A Certain Man" who was arrested in Ireland with several co-conspirators for murdering a land-lord-farmer. While the others were executed, this Certain Man was spared his life —the implication, Kelly understands, being that the Certain Man is his father, and that he turned against his mates, the worst crime a Kelly can commit. O'Neill also tells Kelly about seeing Red Kelly crossing a field one night wearing a woman's dress. Later in the novel, Kelly finds out more about this episode of apparent cross-dressing. Following a stint in prison for a crime his son commits—and attempts to confess to—Red dies, seemingly broken by his most recent incarceration.

George King

King is Ellen Kelly's third husband. He is Kelly's age, and like Kelly he is a sometime horse thief. Ellen bears King's son John at about the same time that Mary Hearn, who will later bear Kelly's daughter, has a child by King as well. Kelly does not discover this connection until much later.

John King

John King is the son of George King and Ellen Kelly.

Jack Lloyd

Jack Lloyd is Ellen Kelly's brother-in-law, married to her sister Kate. He turns Harry Power in to the police and allows people to think that Kelly did it.

Tom Lloyd

Tom Lloyd is Jack's son and Kelly's cousin. For a period he and Kelly are best friends.

Kate Lloyd

Kate is Ellen Kelly's sister and Jack Lloyd's wife.

Constable Tom Lonigan

Tom Lonigan is the first policeman killed, by Kelly, in the incident at Stringybark Creek, which sets off the manhunt for Kelly and his gang.

R. R. McBean

McBean is a magistrate and landowner who is very often Kelly's tormentor and victim. Kelly frequently crosses McBean's Kilfeera Station.

Jack McMonigle

When twenty-one men are arrested following the incident at Stringybark Creek for simply knowing Kelly, McMonigle is among them despite being well-known for having publicly denounced Kelly.

Patchy Moran

Patchy Moran is Kelly's childhood bully. Moran overhears and spreads the tale that O'Neill tells Kelly about seeing Kelly's father in a dress.

Superintendent Nicolson

Nicolson interrogates Kelly in Melbourne, playing the good cop to his partner Hare's bad cop.

Constable O'Neill

O'Neill is the policeman who hangs around the Kelly home early in the novel. He tells Kelly the story about "A Certain Man" and later about seeing Red Kelly in a dress.

Harry Power

Harry Power is a notorious bushranger and outlaw who courts Ellen Kelly and then makes a deal with her to apprentice Kelly in banditry. He becomes both a father figure and nemesis, or adversary, to Kelly, lying to the boy and leading him into deeper and deeper trouble. It is with Power that Kelly commits his first robbery, setting him on the path that will take him finally to his death at Glenrowan.

Jimmy Quinn

Jimmy Quinn is Ellen Kelly's brother and Kelly's uncle. Jimmy is easily provoked, and he is partly responsible for several incidents that end in arrests.

Margaret Quinn

Margaret is Pat Quinn's wife and Ellen Kelly's sister-in-law.

Pat Quinn

Pat Quinn is Ellen Kelly's brother. He is known as Wild Pat the Dubliner and likes to drink to excess.

Edward Rogers

Rogers is a pub owner who intervenes in the fist fight between Wild Wright and Kelly and arranges a public boxing match instead.

J. P. Rowe

Rowe is a squatter, or landowner, from Mount Batten Station, who turns in sixteen-year-old Kelly after seeing him steal a horse.

Dicky Shelton

Dicky Shelton is saved from drowning by the

twelve-year-old Kelly. This is the first time the reader sees the pleasure Kelly takes in helping others.

Aaron Sherritt

Sherritt is Joe Byrne's childhood friend and fellow opium addict. He betrays Byrne and Kelly to the police.

Bill Skilling

Skilling is a miner hired by Ellen Quinn as farm help. He becomes Kelly's brother-in-law when he marries Maggie Kelly.

Detective Michael Ward

Ward is a sadistic detective who tries to intimidate Mary Hearn into telling him what she knows about Kelly's whereabouts.

Dummy Wright

Dummy Wright is Wild Wright's deaf-mute brother. Kelly uses him to provoke a fight with Wild.

Wild Wright

Kelly believes Wright is responsible for charges against Kelly that lead to a jail sentence. The two men fight and later become friends.

Mr. Zinke

Zinke is a lawyer hired by Power to get Kelly out of prison following the robbery incident with Ah Fook.

Post-Colonialism

Colonialism is the use of economic, political, and social policies to maintain or extend control over jurisdictions and peoples that lie outside the nation exercising such power. In the second half of the nineteenth century, the era in which *True History of the Kelly Gang* is set, Australia was struggling to emerge from its colonial past with England and from its own history as a penal colony where English and Irish criminals were sent. In *True History of the Kelly Gang*, the tension this effort generates is made evident in the endless conflicts between the mostly Irish selection-holders, or homesteaders, and the English squatters, landlords who own the larger tracts of property. More particularly, the conflict is evident in the constant, almost daily disputes that pit the Kellys and the Quinns against the local police force, which is staffed by and represents the interests of the English. Ned Kelly is highly alert to the perceived English superiority, and he alludes to it often. While in custody at the Benalla Police Station, he observes that Superintendent Hare is "posh spoken[, sitting] grimly behind the cedar desk trying to frighten me with his blue English eyes.... When he stood up it were like seeing a tapeworm uncurl in your presence." By the end of the novel, Kelly's struggle has enlarged to include a recognizable political dimension. He says this of the relationship between his gang and the poor, Irish, and dispossessed of Australia: "[W]e was them and they was us and we had showed the world what convict blood could do. We proved there were no taint we was of true bone blood and beauty born."

The Outlaw as Hero

Who cheers on the outlaw? Certainly not those who hold and wield power; by definition the outlaw is working against those interests. Across time and cultures, it is the poor with whom the outlaw's adventures resonate; for example, Robin Hood in England, Jesse James in the United States, Pancho Villa and his peasant armies in Mexico, and Phoolan Devi, the "Bandit Queen" in India. All were cheered on by farmers, miners, and others working menial jobs, for whom the outlaw represented an opportunity to retell their own stories, reshape the myths they believed about themselves, and participate in heroism. Outlaws stand up for the oppressed and fight back against the oppressor. For many Australians in the late 1870s, particularly those of Irish descent, Ned Kelly was exactly such a figure—one on whom the aspirations of an entire class could be pinned.

Because Australia was founded as a penal colony and many of its citizens carried the "taint" of convict blood, Kelly's story is particularly potent. Peter Carey's Kelly certainly recognizes the importance of stories people tell about themselves and their history, especially in the case of a people who have been denied a sense of history: "That is the agony of the Great Transportation that our parents would rather forget what come before so we currency lads is left alone ignorant as tadpoles spawned in puddles on the moon." This understanding is the real impetus, or inspiration, for Kelly to commit his story to paper for his unborn daughter. In the first paragraph of the first "parcel" Kelly writes,

> I lost my own father at 12 yr. of age and know what it is to be raised on lies and silences my dear daughter … this history is for you and will contain no single lie may I burn in Hell if I speak false.

Home and Domesticity

Although Ned Kelly at times seem to enjoy the mythical aura developing around him—especially late in *True History of the Kelly Gang*, once his trajectory has been fully established—he never fully embraces it, either. Kelly believes he is the victim of fate, of circumstances completely beyond his control: he was born to Irish parents in Australia; he is falsely accused of crimes he did not commit; and he is apprenticed to the bush-ranger Harry Power. As Kelly repeatedly tells the reader in a number of different ways, all he ever really wanted was a place to settle down and make a quiet life. In fact, it is for love of his home and family, and out of desire for a quiet and trouble-free life, that Kelly commits his first crime, killing a neighbor's calf so that the family has something to eat.

The most obvious and consistent pattern in the novel is that of Kelly's forced removals from and attempts to return to his home. Upon one such return and finding that the farm and his family are both in disarray, Kelly says, "All my life all I wanted were a home." Similar thoughts occur to him often, whenever he feels most estranged from his family and from society. On the other hand, he is able to make a home of sorts in the natural world, in the bush around Power's old cabin at Bullock Creek. His language when he describes moving across the plains or through the Wombat and Warby mountain ranges is so evocative that it is difficult to believe he does not quite feel at home there: "I never seen this country before it were like a fairy story landscape the clear and windy skies was filled with diamonds the jagged black outlines of the ranges were a panorama."

Topics for Further Study

- It has been remarked by critics that *True History of the Kelly Gang* seems to be at least partially indebted to novels and films about the American West. Watch Sam Peckinpah's classic 1973 movie *Pat Garrett and Billy the Kid*. Write a one-page paper comparing Peckinpah's Billy to Peter Carey's Ned Kelly. Consider and compare these two characters' motivation for their actions.

- Ned Kelly is so popular in Australia that muffler shops and burger stands are named after him. Though some Australians are ashamed of his legacy, many still see Kelly as a hero to the oppressed. What does Kelly do in the novel that might account for his ongoing status as a folk hero? Write a five-paragraph essay explaining Kelly's legacy to someone who has never heard of him. Use at least three specific examples from the book as evidence.

- Ned Kelly says his history will "contain no single lie may I burn in Hell if I speak false." But is Kelly an entirely reliable, truthful narrator? In *True History of the Kelly Gang* the reader is presented with only one point of view—that of the storyteller. First-person narrators can alter their stories to cover up mistakes and embarrassing incidents, or make themselves look better than they really are. Write a one-page paper explaining how the other side might view Kelly. How would a policeman's or government official's account of Kelly's activities differ from Kelly's parcels?

- Ned's writing is largely unpunctuated and frequently ungrammatical, but it has an urgency and vibrancy that demand the reader's attention. Write a two-page short story or a fourteen-line poem in the voice of someone you know well who does not speak the same way you do. Be respectful, and try to really listen to the person as you write. What does his or her speech tell you about that person? What does listening tell you about yourself?

- The epigraph to the novel is from William Faulkner's *Absalom, Absalom!*: "The past is not dead. It is not even past." Why does Carey use this for his epigraph? What does this quote mean, and what are its implications? Write a one-page essay explaining how the quote is relevant to the story of Ned Kelly.

Epistolary Novel

True History of the Kelly Gang is an epistolary novel, one in which the story is carried forward by letters written by one or more of the characters. Although, strictly speaking, what Ned Kelly writes are not letters but bound parcels, the novel is in effect one long letter to his unborn daughter.

The effect of an epistolary novel is to impart a sense of immediacy and verisimilitude, or the appearance of truth and realism in fiction or drama. It accomplishes this because Kelly's letters are written in the thick of the action, with no time to even punctuate sentences. Contributing to this sense are the librarian's careful notes at the beginning of each parcel, such as note at the beginning of Parcel 13: "*On page 7 the manuscript is abruptly terminated.*" Carey has placed a note at the beginning of the novel suggesting that the manuscript can be found at the Melbourne Public Library under a particular call number, but there is no actual library of that name. In addition, the use of the epistolary form places the action of the novel even more convincingly in the nineteenth century, as epistolary novels were a common form of literature at that time.

Most importantly, what *True History of the Kelly Gang* gains in its use of the epistolary form is the uninterrupted and unfiltered voice of Ned Kelly. The text is rendered as he himself spoke, in the language and with the word choices of a perceptive and sensitive, if not formally educated, Irish Australian man of the nineteenth century. It is largely unpunctuated and at times poetic. Carey based Kelly's voice in the novel on an existing document, the "Jerilderie Letter," an 8300-word document by the real, historical Ned Kelly, in which he tells of his exploits and the reasons for his actions.

Picaresque Novel

In addition to being an epistolary novel, *True History of the Kelly Gang* is also a picaresque novel. The picaresque novel is usually structured in episodes, not unlike a television or radio show, and tells the story of a rogue, or rascal, who makes his living by his wits rather than through ordinary employment. Often times, these novels are autobiographical. The picaresque form dates to ancient Rome. One of its most best-known examples is Miguel de Cervantes's *Don Quixote*.

Folktale

True History of the Kelly Gang is a kind of folktale, a narrative that develops over the course of many years through repeated retellings. Although the story of Ned Kelly is not properly a folktale— because folktales usually deal with myths, legends, fables and tall-tales—it nevertheless incorporates some elements of the folktale. Kelly's story has been passed along orally as much as in written form, leaving open the probability of cumulative authorship, where each teller contributes something to the story. Also like a folktale, it tells the story of a larger-than-life character who accomplishes tremendous deeds, though in this case the character was a real person and not fictional.

The Great Transportation

Britain began sending its convicted criminals to Australia and surrounding islands in 1788 and continued to do so until 1868, when the last prisoners arrived. By that time, over 150,000 convicts had been "transported." More than a third of them were Irish, like Ned Kelly's parents, and almost all of them came from the lower classes. Very early on, as the convicts completed their sentences and were released, they came into conflict with squatters, freemen who were granted rights to almost limitless tracts of land to raise grazing livestock. Because the convicts were mostly unskilled and uneducated—only half could read and write—there were few opportunities open to them, and the task of building a new society proved difficult. Like any free people, they wanted land, opportunities, and rights. The squatters opposed this, and so hostilities developed between the two groups. The squatters hoarded the land as much as possible, claiming more and more from what had been the "commons," or public lands for the use of all. They impounded stray farm animals that wandered from the former convicts' farms, heightening the existing tensions between the two groups. This situation pitting the ex-convicts and their descendants, especially the Irish convicts, against the English squatters is the source of nearly all Kelly's problems in *True History of the Kelly Gang*. For instance, R. R. McBean's vast landholdings seem to lie between Kelly and wherever he wants to go, surrounding and nearly engulfing Kelly and his family.

Australian Lore

Carey begins *True History of the Kelly Gang* with an epigraph—an inscription on the title page— from American author William Faulkner's novel, *Absalom, Absalom*!: "The past is not dead. It is not even past." With that, Carey appears to be making a case for Ned Kelly's story having some ongoing relevance for modern readers. Although Carey has lived in New York for a number of years, he experienced two formative events, both of which occurred in the 1960s in Australia, that led him to fictionalize the true story of Kelly, a story Carey has called a "powerful foundation myth." First, he saw a series of paintings by artist Sydney Nolan with Ned Kelly as their subject. Later, he read Kelly's fifty-six-page "Jerilderie Letter," the document in which the historical Kelly tries to explain his actions, what drove him, and what he wished for the future even on the eve of his capture and execution. Carey says that Australians still respond to this story so powerfully because Kelly was neither debased nor broken by his experiences, and that he was in a sense triumphant—qualities Australians value even today and which continue to influence the way they think about themselves and their countrymen.

Critical Overview

Peter Carey's *True History of the Kelly Gang* was published simultaneously by Faber and Faber in the United Kingdom and by Knopf in the United States in January 2001. The novel received almost universally favorable reviews in Australia, the United States, and the United Kingdom, from reviewers writing for mainstream publications as well as those writing for a more academic audience.

Almost all of those reviewers remarked upon what Anthony Quinn, writing in the *New York Times Book Review*, called Carey's "fully imagined act of historical impersonation." Quinn is here referring to Carey's deft channeling of the voice he first encountered in the historical Ned Kelly's "Jerilderie Letter," the bushranger's own handwritten and wildly poetic account of his exploits, which Carey adopts and adapts to suit his own purposes in *True History of the Kelly Gang*.

While the last section of the novel is certainly driven by plot, most of the first part of the book seems episodic, with events only loosely linked one to another. Many critics have felt that this does not matter. As Thomas Jones put it in the *London Review of Books*, "The first two thirds of the novel is driven not by the shape of the narrative—it is too fragmented and disconnected for that—but by the blood pressure of the prose. The language is rich but never cloying; the unpunctuated syntax virtuoso."

Some reviewers have registered mild complaints. Besides calling *True History of the Kelly Gang* "an undeniably impressive novel ... a stylistic tour de force," Douglas Ivison in the *Journal of Australian Studies* also addresses what he considers a flaw: that Carey never addresses the larger social and political implications of Kelly's status as a folk hero. Ivison points out that the "contradictions in Kelly's character ... go largely unexamined," and that Kelly, despite the gritty realism evinced in Carey's prose, "remains in the world of romantic myth."

Complaints such as those have been few, and *True History of the Kelly Gang* has succeeded both critically and commercially—it won the 2001 Booker Prize and has so far been Carey's best selling book. "Even if Australian critics are ashamed of Ned Kelly," John Banville writes in the *New York Review of Books*, "they can still take nothing but pride in Peter Carey."

What Do I Read Next?

- Michael Ondaatje's novel *The Collected Works of Billy the Kid* (1970) is similar to *True History of the Kelly Gang* in that Ondaatje writes, at times, from the outlaw's point of view. In form, it intersperses journalism with poetry and autobiography, using a number of different narrators.

- *Jack Maggs* (1997), by Peter Carey, is also a historical novel. It is not set in Australia but one of its central characters is transported as a convict before returning to England.

- Ron Hansen's *The Assassination of Jesse James by the Coward Robert Ford* (1983) tells the fictionalized story of the American outlaw who, like Ned Kelly, was a hero to some and a criminal to others.

- *Wainewright the Poisoner* (2000), a novel by Andrew Morton, tells the story of a famous nineteenth-century prisoner who was transported to Tasmania. Like *True History of the Kelly Gang*, it is written in the form of an apologia, or an explanation for why Wainewright did what he did.

- Winner of the 1993 PEN/Faulkner

Award, Annie Proulx's *Postcards* (1993) is the story of Loyal Blood and his family in the mid-1900s. After Loyal accidentally kills his girlfriend, he is forced to roam about the United States, separated from his family and never truly finding a place to call home.

- Cormac McCarthy's *All the Pretty Horses* (1993) follows the journey of John Grady Cole and his friend Lacey Rawlins as they cross the Mexican border in search of adventure. They find love, death, fear, joy, capture, and redemption in this coming of age novel.

Sources

Banville, John, "The Wild Colonial Boy," in *New York Review of Books*, Vol. 48, No. 5, March 29, 2001, pp. 15-16.

Carey, Peter, *True History of the Kelly Gang*, Vintage International, January 2002.

Gaile, Andreas, "Peter Carey, True History of the Kelly Gang," in *Meanjin*, Vol. 60, No. 3, Sept 1, 2001, pp. 214-19.

Huggan, Graham, "Cultural Memory in Postcolonial Fiction: The Uses and Abuses of Ned Kelly," in *Australian Literary Studies*, Vol. 20, No. 3, May 2002, pp. 142-56.

Ivison, Douglas, Review of *True History of the Kelly Gang*, in *Journal of Australian Studies*, Issue 71, December 15, 2001, pp. 144-45.

Jones, Thomas, "Full Tilt," in *London Review of Books*, February 8, 2001, pp. 24-25.

McCrum, Robert, "Reawakening Ned," *The Observer*, www.books.guardian.co.uk/ (January 7, 2001).

Quinn, Anthony, "Robin Hood of the Outback," in *New York Times Book Review*, January 7, 2001, p. 8.

Further Reading

Drewe, Robert, *Ned Kelly*, Penguin Books, 2004.

Drewe's novel about Ned Kelly is considered the first on the subject of this legendary Australian. His account of Kelly's life was adapted into the 2003 movie *Ned Kelly*.

Hugh, Robert, *The Fatal Shore: The Epic of Australia's Founding*, Vintage, 1988.

First published in 1986, The Fatal Shore tells the story of Australia's founding and history as a penal colony for English and Irish convicts.

Flannery, Tim F., *The Explorers: Stories of Discovery and Adventure from the Australian Frontier*, Grove Press, 2000.

The Explorers is a collection of first-person accounts about the discovery and exploration of Australia, from early accounts in the 1600s to recent stories of adventures still to be had in the continent's outback.

Kelly, Ned, "*Jerilderie Letter*," Alex McDermott, ed., Faber and Faber Ltd., 2001.

Peter Carey was inspired to write *True History of the Kelly Gang* after reading Kelly's original letter stating the motives, purpose, and hopes behind his actions.